MARKETING TIPS FROM JESUS NO ONE WANTS YOU TO KNOW!

Secrets to Growing your Business and Resurrecting your Brand

by Larry C. Lewis

Featured in "Known" by best-selling author Mark Schaefer

Copyright © 2017 by Larry C. Lewis

All rights reserved. In accordane with the U.S. Copyright Act of 1976, the scanning, uploading, and electronic sharing of any part of this book without the permission of the publisher is unlawful piracy and theft of the author's intellectual property. If you woul like to use material from the book (other than for review purposes), prior written permission must be obtained by contacting the publisher at larry@marketinglikeapro.net. Thank you for the support of the author's rights.

This publication is designed to provide accurate information in regard to the subject matter covered. It is sold with the understanding that neither the ahor nor the publisher is engaged in rendering legal, accounting, or other porofessional service. If legal advice or other expert assistance is required, the services of a competent professional person should be sought. – From a Declaration of Principles jointly adopted by a Committee of the American Bar Association and a Commiteee of Publishers.

Market Pro

www.marketinglikeapro.net

First Edition: June 2017

Publisher is not responsible for websites (or their content) that are not owned by the publisher:

Cover, Interior Layout and Design by Digital Exponents
www.digitalexponents.com

Cover image: Anthony Michael Garcia - Fyerbrand

Library of Congress Cataloging-in-Publication Data

Lewis, Larry C.

Marketing Tips From Jesus, No One Wants You To Know: Secrets to Growing your Business and Ressurrecting your Brand

Larry C. Lewis – 1st ed.

ISBN - 978-1-387-03097-2
ISBN - 978-1-387-03096-5

I dedicate this to all the people who believe and never give up because they know one day their dreams will come true. I dedicate this to my amazing kids that always see me as a hero no matter how many times I fail.

I dedicate this to my dear friends Lonna, JT, Carlos, Rico, Will, and John. And to the woman who challenges me and puts a smile on my face every day, Elizabeth.

This is for you!

Contents

Intro	It's So Obvious	5
Chapter 1	**Starting Small** *Go Big and Go Home*	10
Chapter 2	**Building Status** *Power of Network Effects*	19
Chapter 3	**Choosing Your Team** *A Kingdom Divided*	35
Chapter 4	**The Art of Storytelling** *Do People Get You?*	43
Chapter 5	**Consumer Behavior** *Do You Get People?*	52
Chapter 6	**Be Exclusive** *Everyone Else Will Find You Anyway*	60
Chapter 7	**Avoid Competition** *Seek Peace and Pursue It*	64
Chapter 8	**Exploiting New Markets** *Scaling Up*	72
Chapter 9	**Technology** *There's a Better Way*	79
Outro	Rebellion	89

Intro

It's So Obvious

The guru has lied. He's after your money, time, and attention… he wants your commitment. He makes you think he knows something you don't to keep you coming back looking for more.

What are these so-called secrets, and when do they end?

Truth

Nobody knows how to sell! It's impossible to make people buy what they don't want. You can force, trick, or even lie, but you can't make anyone buy anything. Even in the exchange of goods, if the buyer doesn't believe in the product, you still haven't sold anything.

REAL sales happen when you have a product or service people believe in—not just because you sold them something. Money is only paper. Time is currency, attention is currency, action is currency, and consumers have to decide which is more important: Your product or their currency. The outcome depends on the market and how well it's educated about your product. If people are willing to buy, you don't have to sell anything. Tesla doesn't beg anyone to buy their electric cars because everyone wants one... but this isn't true for Chevy.

Even if people do want your product, is demand high enough to create a sustainable business? Engineering students in New York may be enthusiastic about a museum concept in honor of Nikola Tesla, but if you can't convince outsiders it's a valuable product, the idea will fail (as did the Tesla Museum).

Your niche is your fire and your product's the fuel. Your idea must transcend a niche, otherwise it will burn itself out and die.

Most people start what they can't finish, or lack the discipline to stop promoting a bad idea. Rules and exceptions exist for everything in life. Once you understand the rules, you can exceptionally break them. And that's what this book is all about.

Blasphemy

The "gurus" go about chanting how they've discovered something new, something no one knows. But the only thing these gurus are good at is hyping their own products. Hype can only get you so far. Sooner or later, the market will figure you out, and when they do, GAME OVER. You'll never fool them again.

Like it or not, there are conventions to everything.

Hate it or love it, we are all marketers.

We're all selling something. Whether people buy or not is a different story.

Secrets

This stuff has been around for centuries, yet somehow we keep getting it wrong.

Microsoft got it right. Moses got it right. Amazon got it right. America got it right. And Jesus, a man that went as far as to influence time and almost every major religion known to man, he got it right!

So what are we getting wrong?

Well, let me give you the bad news first: Everything is hidden.

The good news: It's all hidden in plain sight. There are no secrets.

Chapter 1

Starting Small
Go Big and Go Home!

Overzealousness is the common plague infecting entrepreneurs all over. Go big or go home, right? Yep, you'll probably be going home. It's good to be ambitious, but you can't achieve all your goals in one fell swoop. Don't forget, Apple started with one product and one customer. They didn't spend mounds of cash on PR or advertising, they targeted a small electronics retailer and delivered a product that gave them industry credibility. Starting small isn't an accident. It's very intentional—even when you have the resources to go big. Redbox was founded by McDonald's and first launched in Denver. After making product improvements—by discontinuing sales of food and beverages in kiosks—Redbox expanded to five more cities only three years after its inception.

This trend is nothing new. It's been around for centuries. Look at Christianity, a product the whole world knows about, yet it started small… very small.

Jesus began his ministry with 12 disciples all from the same city (except Judas), who practiced the same very strict religion. This was his niche market if you will. He spent three years with 12 disciples, nurturing and building relationships with them. Three years, 12 followers.

When you start small, you give yourself the opportunity to learn more about your product, market, and what people expect from a brand like yours. The same way McDonald's tested its Redbox kiosks in Denver, you should test your ideas. Once you learn more about the market, you can make adjustments so your products are better received. Redbox started with DVDs and food in their kiosks. But once they learned customers weren't interested in snacks, they eliminated the food program and invested more into DVD rentals.

Starting small is also a way to recruit enthusiastic fans. Your first converts are the most essential. In marketing we call them "early adopters." These are people willing to give your brand a chance while you are still a nobody, an unknown! Since you aren't a large brand, you probably don't have the resources to pour into a large number of people. So it's best to develop relationships with a small audience, empowering them to promote your product for you. This is how you create brand ambassadors, or as Jesus called them, "disciples." Making disciples is about duplicating yourself, giving you the ability to reach, teach, and sell more.

Brand ambassadors are your partners, they believe in you so much, they'll promote your products for free. Ambassadors are your unpaid sales force, ready to do anything for the sake of the brand.

So educate, empower, and commission your disciples. They will help your brand gain the momentum it needs to grow.

The disciples who were dispersed started spreading the good news about Jesus wherever they went. (Acts 8:4)

Targeting the Right People

Next, you want to make sure you're targeting the right people. This can take some testing. When Snap started, their focus was Stanford students; however, the startup couldn't seem to gain the momentum it needed to grow. Months later, there was a surprising spike in app downloads. But this spike didn't come from Snap's intended audience. The people engaged were high school students, looking for a way to chat privately, away from the watchful eye of parents.

That's why it's important not to waste time on people that don't want your product. You shouldn't have to force your product on anyone. Being a beggar isn't the position you want to be in. Marketing is when people willingly buy your products; it doesn't take force. Some call it "sales." But real sales happen when people see value in your product and happily buy. Apple doesn't beg anyone to buy iPhones, but this isn't the case for Blackberry RIM.

If nobody wants what you're selling, you either have a bad product or you're targeting the wrong people. This is something you have to figure out and change.

THE LYNDA.COM STORY: Lynda Weinman had a vision for a different kind of school. She thought education should be about teaching people what they wanted to learn as opposed to forcing them into a linear school system. In 1995 she founded Lynda.com, a site she calls a "library with videos" for web design books. When she decided to expand, she brought in teachers with expertise in 3D and animation, audio, business, design, development, home computing, photography, video, and web and interactive design. However, she first marketed the concept to students that attended her digital design school and fans of her web design books.

Family First

Don't try to win everyone. Jesus himself targeted a small group of Jews. Targeting everyone at once isn't the best way to use your resources. You have to first capture your primary audience. After that, you'll have the momentum you need to expand to other markets.

Jesus started with 12 disciples, then 12 became 72. If we do the math, that's six new followers for every disciple. Going from 12 to 72 is a convincing sign of exponential growth. 72 disciples equals more promotion, more awareness, and more people wanting more. At this rate, 72 becomes 360, 360 becomes 1800, and 1800 becomes 9000. This is exponential growth… it's fast and hard to stop. This is the kind of momentum you need to promote your business.

Exponential growth happens when every follower attracts at least 1.2 new followers. Jesus exceeded that amount by six times. To keep this momentum going, he didn't allow his followers to get distracted. He kept them focused and gave them specific instructions.

Go! I am sending you out like lambs among wolves. Do not take a purse or bag or sandals; and do not greet anyone on the road. When you enter a house, first say, 'Peace to this house.' If someone who promotes peace is there, your peace will rest on them; if not, it will return to you. Stay there, eating and drinking whatever they give you, for the worker deserves his wages. Do not move around from house to house. (Luke 10:4-7)

Everyone Is Not Your Friend

When starting something new, entrepreneurs have the tendency to market to everyone, hoping to find some kind of traction. You have to first identify your core audience, a niche, a group of early adopters to help you promote your ideas.

This takes time, discipline, and dedication, but it's crucial to your growth. So figure out the kind of people that are willing to embrace your ideas. Spend time with them, nurturing and making them ambassadors for your brand. This kind of tilling will pay off. This makes growing your organization much easier as these following examples show.

Amazon: Amazon started as an online book retailer with plans to expand into other markets in the future. In order to gain momentum, Amazon disciplined itself and concentrated on book enthusiasts. Later, they expanded into other markets including music, movies, and gaming. Now they represent all markets as the "everything store."

Groupon: Groupon started as a one-page site that offered two-for-one pizza deals. Once they gained momentum in the pizza industry, they explored other markets. Groupon is known as one of the fastest growing companies in history. In the beginning they failed and had to start over. But when they started over, they were sure to start small.

Chapter 2

Building Status
Power of Network Effects

Starting small gives you the opportunity to build relationships with your core audience, perfect your offer, and work out the flaws in your business model. It also grants you the time needed to build trust and establish yourself as a serious contender in your market.

"Do not go among the Greeks or enter any town of the Samaritans. Go rather to the lost sheep of Israel. (Matthew 10:5-6)

Apple headquarters used to be a garage, Airbnb was a living room, Disney was a Kansas City attic. After testing their products against a small audience, these organizations were able to improve their value proposition. They learned what the market expected, what they would reject, and what they were willing to accept. The more they learned about the market, the better their products became. Get your niche excited and others are sure to follow. Jesus went after Jews only, Greeks and Romans came on their own.

"Now there were some 'Greeks' among those who went up to worship at the festival. They came to Philip with a request. 'Sir,' they said, 'we would like to see Jesus.'" (John 12:20-21)

"When Jesus reached Capernaum, a centurion came to him, asking for help". (Matthew 8:5)

If you build it, they may not come. But when people are hanging out the doors and windows of your brand, outsiders are sure to come see what's going on.

In marketing, we call this "network effects." When many people gravitate towards a product or service, others naturally follow in fear of missing out.

Are You Competent?

Jesus was challenged on many occasions. People wanted to see if what they heard was true. His enemies, however, were looking for a way to discredit him.

Your organization will face the same kind of challenges. While you are small, you will be ignored for the most part. You won't seem like much of a threat…which is perfect.

Building quietly is a strategy. It's not ideal to draw much attention while your organization is still small. You may be too weak to defend yourself against larger opponents. More established brands have money and resources to destroy brands like yours. They're always paranoid about smaller organizations rising up and taking their position in the marketplace. In the beginning stages of building your brand, you don't need enemies to distract and pull on your resources. All focus should be on growth and fighting should be avoided at all cost.

Jesus' campaign lasted three years. In those years, he taught and performed miracles. Nevertheless, he didn't start teaching until he gave his companions a sign. His first miracle was turning water into wine. Jesus did this to get people's attention. He knew if he didn't have status, he didn't have credibility, and people would not listen. Again, his campaign was three years long. The first two he spent establishing his brand. It wasn't until the last year, and more specifically the last week of his life, that he started to attract haters.

Make some goals, build status, stay quiet about it.

All the Chief Priests and Teachers of the Law called a meeting and said, "What are we going to do about this Jesus? He does many miracles and signs for people to see. If we let him continue like this then the whole nation of Israel will believe in him." (John 11:47-48)

Nobody's Listening

To be taken serious, status is needed. Without status no one will hear you. And if no one can hear you, there's no reason to promote. No one will listen.

Maybe you're already an established player in your industry, or have been successful in other markets. But any time you start something new, you have to prove you are competent and capable of doing what you promise.

You may think you know your niche, but it's not until you dive in that you truly understand what's needed.

Starting small is important because there's always a learning curve. When you GO BIG, you leave yourself vulnerable to larger brands. When you start small, however, your battles are smaller. And if you fail, the market is more forgiving. You are permitted to fail.

Sell, Don't Promote

When you overhype your products, there's no room for error. If expectations are high due to excessive promotion, you're not allowed to make mistakes. You have to deliver!

Joost is a company founded by the owners of Skype, and was supposed to be what Netflix is today. With more funding than both Netflix and Hulu, Joost spent most of its assets on marketing, advertising, and PR. But when their product hit the market, it underperformed. It was far from what they had promised.

If you draw a lot of attention to your product, it better be good! Otherwise, you will be seen as incompetent, incapable of delivering on your promise. A brand is established on its promise. If you say one thing and do another, the market will lose faith in you, and it will be next to impossible to reestablish your brand.

Without Trust, You Have No Brand

Joost promised an amazing video-sharing platform that would revolutionize the way we consume entertainment. After the product launched, however, the technology caused the content to be inaccessible. When the bugs were finally worked out, no one even wanted it for free. Soon after, Hulu and NetFlix developed user-friendly solutions. And Joost? Well, have you heard anything? Neither have I.

Joost launched in 2006, and it wasn't until 2007 that Netflix begin its video streaming service. Being the first mover isn't always an advantage. Timing is everything… start humble, fail small, finish last. This is what Apple did with the iPad, iPod, and iPhone. It's what Apple always does.

The Thomas Edison Story: Thomas Edison Didn't Invent The Light Bulb, he just made the best version of it. In Edison's own words he says, "I start where the last man finish".

Last Mover Advantage

Jesus was also a last mover. In Judaism there were many prophets and kings that preceded him. They all spoke about the Anointed One, the Christ, the last mover in Judaism.

Being the last mover is about capitalizing on opportunities everyone else seems to miss. The iPod wasn't the first MP3 player, but it was more user friendly than anything that preceded it. It was also marketed as "1000 songs in your pocket," helping people grasp the concept of a "gigabyte." This is marketing. Although MP3 Man was the first to market, Apple recognized the value, helped the market see it, and made it easy for consumers to capture it [the value]. Something similar was done with Apple music. Napster was the first mover, then Kazaa and other copycats followed. But Apple used marketing to position itself as a leader by building relationships with music executives and making it easy for users to access MP3's "legally."

Every business should aim to be the last mover in its industry just as the Christ, the Savior, the Anointed One.

When starting something new, building awareness is key, and

great marketing needs little promotion. If people know it exists, the product will carry itself, given that the offer is good.

Without Status You Have No Voice

While two people can sell the same exact thing, one will fail and the other succeed. Why is that? It's status, my dear friend.

When Al-Qaeda struck the U.S. after multiple warnings, George Bush's capacity to lead came into question. When Peter Popoff was exposed for performing fake miracles, his ministry folded and he filed bankruptcy.

Trust is a big thing when it comes to promotion. If people can't trust you, you have no brand.

Make all the promises you want. You can even give your product away for free (as we saw with Joost). But if your reputation is tarnished, no one will care. Until you build a reputable brand you're voiceless, you have no seat in the marketplace.

Hitler had ambitions to conquer the world. He started by building alliances with large countries and invaded smaller ones. But he got greedy. Puffed up with all his success, he decided to declare war on Russia, Great Britain, and the United States. This was suicide, which he ultimately committed in 1945.

Muhammad, founder of Islam, was also a military leader that started small and built many alliances through marriages and treaties. There was a time he became so arrogant, he marched on an army 10 times his size. This was called "The Battle of Uhud," where he famously lost a tooth. Faith or stupidity? Given that he lost that battle, I think it's safe to say, that wasn't his smartest move.

Saul, the first king of Israel, also became arrogant; he even turned on his own comrades. His arrogance caused his death and that of his sons, and the rest of his family. Then David, who wasn't even of royal descent, became king. He was humble.

The Bible's Gideon was also humble. Nevertheless, he went up against an army the Bible says couldn't even be counted. Gideon himself had 300 men (similar to the movie "300") and took on several nations. This wasn't an offensive, however; Gideon was only protecting his nation. The arrogant people that came against him failed, kind of like Facebook's war on Snapchat (e.g. Poke, Instagram Stories). And they still can't seem to bury the Snapchat ghost.

Humbleness Is Key

Jesus was born in a manger where cows eat and sleep. Even when his fame spread across the nation of Israel, he remained humble. The Pharisees, the religious leaders of Israel, were very arrogant, however. They were highly educated and dressed in the finest clothing. Jesus was poor and homeless, yet he had more followers than all of them.

Coming to His hometown, He taught the people in their synagogue, and they were astonished. "Where did this man get such wisdom and miraculous powers?" they asked. "Is this not the carpenter's son? Isn't His mother's name Mary, and aren't His brothers James, Joseph, Simon, and Judas? Aren't all His sisters with us as well? Where then did this man get all these things?" (Matthew 13:54-56)

Power of Testimony

Testimonies about your brand are powerful. People no longer believe what you say about yourself. They turn to Facebook, Twitter, and Snapchat to see what others are saying about you. This way, you no longer have to sell yourself. The people you encounter will market your brand for you. Since they have so much faith in what they've "seen you do," they have no problem sharing their experience with the world. This is actually a great reward for them. So it's important to make people want to be associated with your brand through the status you build and the trust you establish with your audience. If they brag about you, you have to deliver. It makes them look good.

Jesus entered Jericho and was passing through. A man was there by the name of Zacchaeus; he was a chief tax collector and was wealthy. He wanted to see who Jesus was, but because he was short he could not see over the crowd. So he ran ahead and climbed a sycamore-fig tree to see him, since Jesus was coming that way. (Luke 19:1-4)

The point of testimonials and reviews is to show people that you are capable of doing what you say you can do. People need to know they can trust you. The first time you heard of Uber or Airbnb you probably wondered, "Why are so many people using these services? How could you trust riding with a stranger or staying in someone's home you've never met?" It's because they started with small groups of users to build trust and credibility. So even if you've never used these applications before, in your time of need, you'll trust the service and use it based on the experience of others.

So build status. It's great for business as these examples show.

Uber: There were many reports about how Uber was a risky service to use. People doubted that a mobile app that helped users find rides with strangers could be safe. Despite all the bad reports, Uber was able to establish itself as a secure and reliable ride sharing service. Nevertheless, if it wasn't for their ability to suppress user fears and prove that it was, in fact, a trusted resource for safe travel, they would have never been able to become the #1 transportation service in the world.

Will Smith: Will Smith made it pretty big in the music industry with his clean, comedic rap style. His rap persona was later featured in the popular TV sitcom, "Fresh Prince of Bel-Air." Later, Smith decided he wanted to be the biggest movie star in the world. But first, he had to establish himself as a Hollywood contender, although he already had status as a rap star. Smith started with little roles in movies such as, "Where The Day Takes You," and "Made in America." But after a few years of studying the film industry and training, he landed a major role in the movie, "Bad Boys." It wasn't until his role in "Independence Day" that he built the status he needed to become a major Hollywood player.

Chapter 3

Choosing Your Team

A Kingdom Divided By Itself Will Fall

I once sat on the board for an organization that specialized in promoting events, and it was one of the most painful experiences I've ever had to endure. There were 12 members total. Everyone got along. Everyone had great ideas. Everyone had different ideas. And nothing got done.

Twelve chiefs in one tribe. That's way too many chiefs. It's very hard to get 12 people to agree on anything, especially when they're from different cultures and have diverse backgrounds.

Take a hint from some of the largest organizations in the world: Facebook has 8 board members, PayPal has 8, Netflix has 9, and Google has 5. It may surprise you, however, that each of these companies started with 4 board members or less. Jesus had 12 Disciples! And somehow this became the magic number for a board of directors. But his 12 Disciples weren't all decision makers. Jesus actually had a board of 4... Himself, Peter, James, and John.

He did not let anyone follow him except Peter, James and John the brother of James. (Mark 5:37)

After six days Jesus took Peter, James and John with him and led them up a high mountain, where they were all alone. (Mark 9:2)

In fact, James, Peter, and John, who were known as pillars of the church, recognized the gift God had given me, and they accepted Barnabas and me [Paul] as their co-workers. (Galatians 2:9)

Are you getting the point?

Too many decision makers can sabotage any real progress. It's better to start with a few key players and maybe a few advisors. It's important that you build a solid cohesive team that is productive. Everyone in your organization should believe in the vision as much as you do. A single weak link can cause the whole chain to break.

Flow

Every organization, especially in the early stages of a campaign, needs something called flow. I usually refer to it as momentum. But it's when your team is so connected that everyone moves as one unstoppable force. It's the no-look pass to Michael Jordan on a fast break as he catches the basketball in mid-air and jams it. It's Navy Seal Team 6 sweeping through Palestine hunting for

Bin Laden. It's chemistry, it's focus, it's determination, and everyone on your team is infected.

With flow, the impossible becomes possible. Space travel was once an inconceivable notion. But when the stakes were high, America assembled Apollo, and eight years later a man was on the moon. No other country in history has put a man on the moon. But when you have flow, nothing is out of reach.

"Look!" the LORD said. "The people are united, and they all speak the same language. After this, nothing they set out to do will be impossible for them! (Genesis 11:6)

Funding

Jesus had a number of disciples that helped fund his ministry. Some of his financial supporters included Matthew (tax collector), Zacchaeus (chief tax collector), Nicodemus (Pharisee), Mary Magdalene, Joanna, Susanna (Luke 8:2-3), and

Joseph (a man the Bible calls rich in Matthew 27:57).

Every campaign needs some source of funding, so don't expect everything to come for free.

Commonalities On Jesus' Team

Jesus' 12 disciples were all fishermen (except for Matthew). Jesus first chose Peter, Andrew, James, and John. Not only were they partners in the fishing industry, they were also brothers (Peter and Andrew, James and John), and from Galilee (except for Judas who betrayed him). Most of them were already friends or related somehow. So they had a lot in common.

Jesus' disciples were very loyal, willing to do anything for Jesus, even die.

"Look," said Peter, "we have left everything we had to follow You." (Luke 18:28)

Your Team Matters

The Dennis Rodman Story: Dennis Rodaman was a bad fit for the San Antonio Spurs -- a conservative team with a good image. When Gregg Popovich joined the organization his main goal was to get Rodman out. After Rodman was ousted and sent to Chicago, the Spurs became a championship team, as well as the Bulls.

Make sure you pick a solid team that can work together without strife. Everyone on your team should believe in the mission and work as one towards a common goal. Everyone should be willing to sacrifice for the greater good, because a house divided by itself will fall.

U.S. Government: Whenever you think of dealings with the

U.S. Government, you think of a long, painful process. There are 535 decision makers in Congress, and sometimes this means that necessary bills and laws never get passed. However, when there's a state of emergency, the U.S. calls on a small group of qualified individuals to make things happen quickly. This has been the "secret sauce" used in every great American innovation, from nuclear bombs to the Internet. After every major problem is solved, however, America passes the technology on to the public and becomes slow again.

One major operation America is known for is "The Skunk Works." This is a team of engineers called on by the government to make miracles happen. Most of their projects are done without contracts or special approval; the U.S. government just gives them a special task to complete it by any means necessary. This gives them the freedom to execute the plan uninterrupted.

PayPal: One of the greatest teams ever put together was a group of nerds known as the "PayPal Mafia." Peter Thiel was the leader of this bunch, and in his book "Zero to One," he explains how he purposely picked a small team of workaholics that believed in his vision and was willing to sacrifice all for the purpose of the mission. One of his goals was to put together a team that would develop relationships even outside of the office. As a result, this team pumped out other successful products including LinkedIn, Yelp, YouTube, SpaceX, Tesla, and Palantir (technology used to track down Bin Laden).

Chapter 4

The Art of Storytelling
Do People Get You?

One of the most important aspects of marketing is storytelling. In order for people to buy your product they have to know what you're selling. Jesus used parables as a way of explaining things that were otherwise difficult to understand.

With many such parables Jesus spoke the word to them, to the extent that they could understand. (Mark 4:33)

But you will find that Jesus used parables to confuse people as well… on purpose. Because some really didn't believe in the product, so Jesus wasted no time selling to them.

The disciples came to him and asked, "Why do you speak to the people in parables?" He replied, "Because the knowledge of the secrets of heaven has been given to you, but not to them." (Matthew 13:10-11)

It's important to separate the wolves from the sheep. Why fatten the sheep for the wolves to devour? You don't have the time or resources to appeal to everyone at once. You have to distinguish between certain groups and approach them separately.

Storytelling can work in two ways: You can intentionally capture your audience and exclude other groups. But not telling your story will isolate everyone.

Storytelling has been around since the beginning of time, often seen in music, oral presentations, dance, and even rock carving. Now we use books, video games, and movies to tell stories. The

Bible is also a story, with narratives dating back 6000 years. There are three elements to every great story, and it's not conflict, climax, or resolution. It's intrigue, suspense, and reward.

Intrigue

If you want people to pay attention, you have to be intriguing. You can create intrigue by saying things people don't expect, or by challenging the norm. For example, Jesus was very intriguing because he always shocked his listeners. He would surprise them by sharing ideas that went against conventional thinking, causing people to imagine something new and exciting.

Donald Trump was very intriguing in his 2016 presidential campaign efforts. He often said things people couldn't believe. And although many were afraid to admit it (because of his bizarre ideas), he generated a lot of secret followers due to his ability to intrigue his listeners.

Once you have someone's attention, they will be open to your ideas. So if your offer seems valuable to the listener, they'll probably buy it. So always think of ways to challenge the norm. Avoid trying to fit in at all cost. Once you create intrigue, you'll have the opportunity to tell your story. And if your story is good, you'll get the sell.

Suspense

In order to hold your listeners attention, you need to create suspense. This means, don't give away the whole story at once. Give people the ability to imagine the outcome. Psychologically, suspense increases the neurotransmitter dopamine levels in the brain, which is the chemical that intensifies desire and want.

Some people call it "the man in the jungle effect." But no matter what you call it, it happens when you create an unlikely scenario, with an outcome that is hard to determine. You see it all the time on TV, when you don't know how your favorite character is going to survive the episode. Suspense will have you hanging on for a week, or even until the next season, just to get the revelation on how the story ends.

Look at all the cliffhangers "The Walking Dead" produces. People hang on weeks, and even months, to get a revelation on a suspense built scenario. Seven seasons in and people are still watching to see how the story unfolds.

Reward

If your story is intriguing people will pay attention. If your story is suspenseful, people will hang on till the end. But what keeps people coming back is the reward.

When people filled arenas to see Michael Jackson perform, they knew they were getting a treat. When Iron Mike Tyson entered the boxing ring, people expected a display of great skill and strength. And when disciples followed Jesus, they were expecting miracles and a display of great wit.

So why do you want people to pay attention to you? What's so great about your story? Why should people follow you? What reward can they expect?

A Good Story Should Be Simple

Leave out all the details that confuse people and add nothing to the plot. Jesus told parables that made it easy for people to understand what he was selling. Too many details can bore your audience. And when you're introducing a new product, you can't afford to lose listeners. Find things that interest them and tell stories from their perspective. It will help you connect with your audience on a personal level.

Don't use large words unless your audience appreciates intellectual speak, because people don't like to feel stupid. In your stories, reference events in the past, present and future. This will help your listeners see where they were, where they are, and where your product will take them.

Abraham Lincoln: Abraham Lincoln's Gettysburg Address was only 272 words and lasted about two minutes. This is known as one of the greatest speeches ever delivered. It was very effective and simple. Lincoln was a self-taught lawyer who was very intellectual. Yet he delivered a simple message with the objective of honoring those who died in the Civil War and gaining more support for it. He started the speech with the history and vision of America, its present state, and what the war would accomplish.

Space X: Elon Musk (CEO of Space X and Tesla) tells stories through public relations and product launch events. To create intrigue he talks about his aspirations to "populate Mars," and other crazy ideas that seem impossible. Some of his short term goals include reusable rockets that will make space travel much cheaper, and rockets that can land in designated landing spaces. The average cost to go to the moon used to be about $30 million. But with SpaceX reusable rockets, the price has dropped to about $8 million. The suspense in his narrative is how he will do it, since he is an entrepreneur with no rocket building experience. Nevertheless, Elon built the first U.S. rocket in 40 years, something NASA hasn't even done. The reward is seeing the live broadcast of his space shuttles taking launch and returning to earth undamaged. His achievements have made him known as the real life "Tony Stark (Iron Man)."

Martin Luther King Jr: Martin Luther King Jr.'s "I Have a Dream" speech is one of the greatest stories ever told. He pointed out the way things were and helped people imagine how things could be. A world without racism was an intriguing plot. His dream was that someday whites and blacks would live in unity. It was a great thing to imagine, and it gave people hope (the reward).

Chapter 5

Consumer Behavior
Do You Get People?

Businesses fail because they don't know how to appeal to human nature. If your product contradicts the organic rhythm of human behavior, it will be difficult to sell anything, no matter how good you promote it.

"Come to me, all you who are weary and burdened, and I will give you rest. Take my yoke upon you and learn from me, for I am gentle and humble in heart, and you will find rest for your souls. For my yoke is easy and my burden is light." (Matthew 11:28-30)

Jesus did multiple things in this quote. He was selling hope, telling people the investment was small, and made it optional for all. Let me show you the powers at work in this proposal.

The Product

If you want people to take action, the best three ways to influence behavior is to offer hope, pleasure, or social acceptance.

According to the Fogg Behavior Model, people are motivated to seek hope and avoid fear, seek pleasure and avoid pain, and seek acceptance and avoid rejection. Most organizations offer one at best. Jesus offers all three, making the motivation to buy high.

But what's so bizarre about his offer, is that it's free, and the effort involved is minimal. You don't have to follow any particular rules or pay money to maintain it. That's intriguing, and that's also what makes it different from every other religion.

There are no rules with the exception of the rule to love. Everything is consistent with natural behavior. People naturally want to love and be loved, give and receive, respect and be respected. But Christianity is no longer Christianity when rules are enforced. It's a religion that asks you to do what you already want to do naturally.

A rule is a form of payment. But when people accept something for free, they feel obligated to give something back in return. Jesus said, "Come and eat without payment." Later, he told his disciples, "Give as you have been freely given."

When someone holds the door for you at a convenience store, in turn you're more willing to hold the door for someone else. If someone lets you cut in at a busy interaction, you are likely to do the same for someone else.

The gift of the gospel is genius. It's free. Nothing is required. But when pastors and leaders try to enforce rules, they make the product hard to sell.

Options

A lot of organizations make the mistake of telling people they "have to" do this, or they "have to" do that. But when you give people the option to do what they already want to do, they'll be willing to do even more.

For example, Jesus didn't force his product on anyone. He gave them the option to accept it or reject it. However, the deal was so sweet (go to heaven for free; all you have to do is let me die for you) most people bought it.

Small Investments

When you offer something valuable for a small investment, it's hard for people to say no. Jesus said, "My yoke is light," suggesting that the reward was much greater than the investment. The investment was so small, it was easy for many to jump on board. And once on board, it's much easier to get them to make other commitments.

In marketing, we call this "the foot in the door effect." Make a small request, and, over time, people will be willing to make greater contributions. Many died for the Gospel. Others gave up their way of life to help spread the news across the world. But never make high demands when starting something new or reviving your brand. Set people at ease by making simple request. Later you can ask for something more dramatic as the following companies did.

PayPal: PayPal gave new customers $10 to try their product. Consumers had fears that exchanging money via the Internet would be unsafe. They worried their private information would be compromised and their accounts hacked. But once PayPal got users to try it, they demonstrated how safe, reliable, and easy their product was to use. Now PayPal is the leading online payment solution in just about every country. They did this by eliminating fears and making the exchange of goods (something people naturally do) much easier.

Candy Crush: Candy Crush Saga is a game you can download for free, but the more you invest your time into it, the more likely you are to buy game enhancements. Though it may seem silly to buy lollipop hammers, the time you invested in the product justifies the purchase. Thus, Candy Crush Saga generates billions of dollars a year in revenue.

Mafia Wars: Although Mafia Wars was a game based on text, it played on psychology and natural human behavior.

1. Naturally, people don't like to pay for stuff they think they don't need. As a result, MW offered its game for free.

2. If people make small investments, they are willing to make larger investments later in the relationship. MW initially got people to invest time. Later people were shocked they spent hundreds—thousands in many cases!—on virtual goods.

3. Naturally, people love to compete. As a result, MW allowed users to compete against friends and family.

4. People love stories. MW allowed users to imagine themselves as real life mobsters.

5. People are social by nature. Prisoners in solitary go crazy! But MW allowed users to recruit family and friends to their online mob organizations.

6. When people don't know what to expect, they keep coming back. Playing Mafia Wars, you often had to check on your organization and react to opposition. Entertainment is a hard industry for user retention. Think about it. After you watch a movie, how often do you go back to see it? The same goes for

music, sports, and games. If you know what to expect, interest dies out. But if a product has variables, something different every time you encounter it, people will return frequently and stay invested.

Chapter 6

Be Exclusive

Everyone Else Will Find You Anyway!

Businesses often make the mistake of trying to market to everyone under the sun. Do you have enough resources to do that? More importantly, do you have the time?

Everyone doesn't have to like your product. But when they see that others do, they're going to want it anyway.

When Donald Trump started his presidential campaign in 2015, he was very exclusive. Although he's liberal like most New Yorkers, he campaigned under the conservative banner. Democrats didn't understand it and Republicans didn't like it. Since when has Donald Trump been conservative? Never. But launching his campaign, he knew he had to be exclusive.

A lot of people think Donald Trump is racist, abusive, and condescending. In my assessment, Trump is wise. He's a businessman, a marketer, and he knows how to influence.

He focused on a niche that was so excited about his campaign they transformed their vehicles to reflect their support. After getting his core fired up he became a little more inclusive. This was toward the end of his campaign, because he needed more than white working class males backing him. He needed the black vote, Hispanic vote, and the woman vote.
But by being exclusive, he built a lot of momentum. It confused some and made others curious, thus, earning him a larger following.

When God raised up his servant, Jesus, he sent him first to the

Jews. (Acts 3:26)

Jesus initially starting with Jews wasn't an accident. Even the first book of the Bible "Genesis" is exclusive. It focused on one family: Abraham his two sons and their mothers. One woman is the mother of Islam, the other is the mother of Christianity. From these women came the two most dominating religions, Islam and Christianity.

Whatever Sarah says to you, listen to her, because your offspring will be traced through Isaac. But I will also make a nation of the slave's son because he is your offspring." (Genesis 21:12-13)

If being exclusive works for religion and politics, what does that mean for your business?

PayPal: PayPal exploited the eBay market to the point it couldn't grow anymore unless it leaked into other markets. The only way PayPal could continue to grow is if eBay grew, or if

PayPal started to explore other markets. eBay's growth leveled off, so PayPal had no choice but to explore other markets. Therefore, they skipped the B2B space and went directly to customers. This is when they started offering $10 to every new user that signed up. Anyone who used the product automatically promoted it, because in order to use PayPal, both parties need an account.

Apple: The iPhone was exclusive to AT&T customers for years. This created desire for non-users. Now Apple owns 40% of the U.S. market, but has been seeing declines due to the rise of Android.

Chapter 7

Avoid Competition

Seek Peace and Pursue It

A lot of organizations make the mistake of entering into direct competition with already established brands. They call it "disruption." But this doesn't work well for small organizations rising up against big corporations with deep pockets.

Competing in an aggressive industry, even if you're a top contender, can take your focus away from the real mission. While Microsoft and Google competed with products like Bing and Google Search, Office and Docs, Explorer, and Chrome, Apple grew larger than both companies combined. But when Apple started competing against Google (Android vs. iOS, Maps vs. Maps), Samsung set up shop and started building a monopoly in the world's largest mobile market, China.

You should never intentionally enter into competition with any organization. In fact, do your best to avoid competition at all cost. Why be distracted by what other people are doing? Shouldn't you be focused on your own organizational goals and objectives? Competition will cost you time, money, and peace. Instead, you should grow your business quietly. Once you become a valid threat, it will be hard to avoid friction. But as long as it depends on you, be at peace with everybody.

How To Build Your Wall

In the United States, Russia's President Vladimir Putin has a very bad image and he is often seen as a bully. But you may be surprised that most Russians actually like him. When he invaded Crimea, many didn't understand it. But what many people don't realize is that many Crimeans actually welcome Russian presence. Is Russia trying to rebuild the USSR? Probably so. Just think, in WWII, Russia lost a lot of real estate that kept the country safe. Without the Ukraine, Russia's border is susceptible to attack. So to ensure safety, Vladimir Putin will need to recapture the Ukraine and use it as a bumper to its border.

The United States does the same thing with rivers, deserts, seas, and land. It would be hard for another country to invade. If they wanted to attack by water, they would have to make it past our Navy that guards every major sea. It's also difficult to strike by air since we own space (unofficially) and have the technology to strike down any air attack. It would also be hard to attack by land since the U.S. is geographically isolated. The only other option is to move through Canada or Mexico, which would be difficult because no one can do it without being noticed. This power and position also gives us the ability to control trade and impose sanctions on other nations.

Just think about the chaos in the Middle East. Those countries have trouble growing because they're always fighting one another. This also makes them less of a threat to the United States. Every country experiences the most growth in times of peace. Just think, America emerged as a super power at the end of two world wars, which we had little involvement in.

Our biggest conflict to date is the Revolutionary War, but we didn't dare stir conflict with Britain until we established our own armies and developed resources. The first Pilgrims came to America in 1620. But it wasn't until 1765 that the United States rebelled against Great Britain. Britain had become weak after the seven-year French and Indian War, while America strengthened and became resourceful.

That's why as a small organization, it's best to avoid conflict.

Grow in silence. Don't startle the big guys. When you're strong enough to defend yourself, they'll take notice, and hopefully they'll be seeking an alliance instead of a war.

Jesus sent messengers on ahead, who went into a Samaritan village to get things ready for him; but the people there did not welcome him, because he was heading for Jerusalem. When the disciples James and John saw this, they asked, "Lord, do you want us to call fire down from heaven to destroy them?" But Jesus turned and rebuked them. (Luke 9:52-55)

Jesus didn't like competition and neither should you.

Fast Food Wars: From McDonald's to Burger King, almost every fast food chain has "4 for 4" deal. Competition is a distraction that forces organizations to fight over products and services that drive margins, prices, and profits down.

The goal for every business is to start small, build trust, and grow silently. By the time the competition catches on, you will be strong enough to defend yourself. Some businesses seek war and fail, others stay quiet and prevail. But it can sometimes be challenging, as the following examples suggest.

Napster: In 1999 Shawn Fanning revealed to some friends in an online chatroom that he was building a revolutionary product that would change the music industry forever. Partnering with Sean Parker, the two raised $50,000 in seed money and headed to Silicon Valley, California. Napster's community grew to 20 million users in only one year, raising antennas from the Record Industry Association of America (RIAA). Feeling threatened by the young team of entrepreneurs, the RIAA filed a lawsuit against Napster for violating copyright laws. However, Napster implored its community to boycott the music industry and stop supporting artists that didn't partner with Napster. As you can see, Napster created a lot of enemies for themselves, but the giant that drove them out of business was the RIAA.

Apple iTunes: Noticing users growing desire to access MP3s, Steve Jobs and his team came up with a plan. They wondered if they created a hub for digital downloads that was safe, easy to use, and reliable, will people actually buy the music? Their assumption was right. But instead of creating enemies for themselves they found allies. Steve Jobs first took his plan to Warner Music and Universal, proposing that he would start off small by selling songs only to Mac users through iTunes. Later other record labels like BMG and Sony hopped on board. This gave them an alternative to their dying CD sales, and also allowed them to recoup some of their losses from peer-to-peer file sharing applications like Napster and MP3.com.

Snap: Snap, creator of Snapchat, grew quietly without much opposition. When Facebook realized they could be a possible threat, they attempted to buy them out. However, Snapchat refused their offer and continued to innovate. Since then, Mark Zuckerberg and Facebook vowed to put an end to Snap with competing products like Poke and Instagram. Facebook's vast resources have proven to be a challenge for Snap and has cut into their market share. Should Snap have taken Facebook's offer? Only time will tell if they will be able to maintain a solid position in the marketplace and remain a significant social network. However, this proves that competition should be avoided at all cost.

Chapter 8

Exploiting New Markets

Scaling Up

In Chapter 7 we talked about how Apple iTunes got started, but I think it's worth sharing how they expanded and exploited other markets.

iTunes started with a small audience of Mac-only users in order to test the product and make improvements. Its playlist consisted of 200,000 of the most popular songs. In its first week, Apple sold over 1 million titles, giving record labels the confidence they needed to feel safe about their service. After six months of continuous progress, Steve Jobs asked the labels if he could expand into other markets by allowing Windows users to purchase music as well (notice "the foot in the door effect"). With full confidence, the record labels agreed.

As iTunes became more and more popular, they considered ways to sell more products. When deciding how to expand or "scale up," there are few things to consider. Will you scale up through new products and services, or will you find more people to buy what you already have? Apple decided to do both.

Not only did Apple add new titles to iTunes (more products), they also found more buyers to access their music library (opening iTunes up to Window users).

Amazon, however, decided to add new products. Instead of finding more people to buy books, they looked for new markets closely related to the products they already offered. For example, Hidden Valley is owned by Clorox, but Clorox doesn't put its name on the package because most people wouldn't buy salad dressing from bleach people. But if your name is on the product, it's best that your offer is closely related to what you already sell. So when iTunes expanded, it did it with movies, TV shows, and apps. When Amazon expanded, it did it with movies, music, and games.

How Do You Plan To Scale Up?

The Gospel is only one product. So the only way to scale up is by finding more buyers. Therefore, Christianity had to expand geographically. And when Jesus finally decided to venture into other markets, he didn't jump from Jerusalem to Costa Rica. He started with his nearest countrymen, Grecian Jews and Samaritans.

Are You Ready?

Something you don't want to do is force a product that is premature into a broad market. That's why we started small remember? We had to build and create momentum by exploiting our niche. Your niche will prepare you for the larger markets. All mistakes made early can be forgiven, but not if you're marketing to a broad audience. Large audiences are less forgiving. We start small in order to grow and build a solid foundation. Jesus was born a baby, but started promoting the gospel when he was 30. When crowds started believing in him, and his fame grew, people got jealous, and that's when he started experiencing the most conflict.

People are threatened by things that are new or different (which your product should be). So it's key to stay quiet about it until you gain a solid position in the market.

Have you ever seen the first Apple computer? It's a piece of junk! It looks like a block of wood carved by hand. Now Apple's products are polished and well designed. But had they glamorized the outside of their product in their early stages, they would have went bankrupt.

Do you think your product is ready to expand into new markets?

Let's find out!

A great persecution broke out against the church in Jerusalem, and all except the apostles were scattered throughout Judea and Samaria... Saul began to destroy the church. Going from house to house, he dragged off both men and women and put them in prison. Those who had been scattered preached the word wherever they went. (Acts 8:1-4)

Strategic Expansion

The gospel message expanded into other markets after three and a half years, similar to the RedBox story from Chapter 1. Their number jumped from 120 followers (according to Acts 1:15) to 3,120 in one day. At this time Christians had so much momentum, they were literally unstoppable, and their growth was exponential because each believer attracted multiple disciples. Remember the rule of exponential growth? If each follower attracts at least 1.2 new followers on average, your organization will experience exponential growth. At this time, however, the disciples refused to go to other nations and remained in Jerusalem until they were forced out.

Alexander The Great Story: When Philip 11 of Macedon died, his son, Alexander the Great, resumed power. However, before marching on any nation, he secured his territory in Greece. Once he solidified his position in his home country, he went east to Asia Minor to invade Persia, his nearest threat. Then he went further east into India, then doubled back west invading Syria, Judea, and Egypt. In Greece he appointed tyrants, but in Asia he encouraged democracy in order to brand himself as a liberator of Persian ruled territories. War is just another campaign. After building your army and securing your niche, you can later expand into the nearest markets, increasing your reach and helping your brand grow.

Apple Newton: The Apple Newton was the first tablet to hit the market in 1987. However, the product flopped. Not only was the product immature, but the market was immature as well.

Nevertheless, in 2010, the new and improved Apple Newton was relaunched as the iPad, and took the whole mobile market by storm.

Chapter 9

Technology

Is There a Better Way?

Do you know any new or better ways to produce products and promote your brand? Are you afraid of trying something new? If so, you shouldn't be. Technology can help you reach and do more than ever before. If you fail to leverage technology others will leave you behind.

Nokia was once a leading information technology and communications company that lost market share when they failed to shift to more efficient ways of producing valuable solutions. In an effort to compete with Google and other data collecting services, Nokia bought Navteq for $8 billion, a company that planted in-road traffic sensors across the United States and Europe. While they were investing in physical infrastructure, a company by the name of Waze was on the rise. However, instead of investing in hardware, Waze created an app that allows smartphone users to submit real time traffic information. This cost Waze almost $0, yet their system is 10 times more efficient. Since Nokia failed to embrace "the better way," they were left behind, and ultimately had to sell Navteq for $3 billion dollars.

Out of fear, organizations refuse to leverage technology. But fear comes from lack of confidence. Kodak lacked the confidence to shift their business model from a print strategy to a digital strategy afraid to leave revenue behind from their film market.

Tesla made the first all-electric car because automakers feared market rejection. They weren't confident enough to take the risk. When it comes to autonomous vehicles (self-driving cars),

Mercedes, GM, Audi, Volvo, Toyota, have all had the technology since the 80s, but only Google had the guts to bring unmanned vehicles to market (2009). It was also Google that replaced human auditors with algorithm updates like Panda and Penguin. While Yahoo held on to its human review system—as if it was a competitive advantage—Google leveraged technology to create the fastest and most efficient search retrieval service. By the time Yahoo made the shift, it was too late. Google had a monopoly and still does.

Are Robots Taking Human Jobs?

Yes, and they should. As the world progresses, so should the human race. McDonald's caught flack when they introduced self-service kiosk to replace cashiers. But in reality, corporations have been using this technology for decades. John Roscoe introduced self-service pumps at his Big Top convenient store in 1964, a technology that replaced human attendants. Banks have done the same with ATMs, retail stores with self-checkout, Panera with tablet kiosks. This is nothing new.

Divorce Your Product, Marry The Market

When Blackberry refused to move from QWERTY keyboards to touch screen technology, they went from 20% market share to 0.6% in four years. That's a huge drop for a $3 billion dollar company. This proves how foolish it is to marry your technology.

Market Demand Transcends Technology

Kodak had a monopoly in the film industry. However, it should have looked at itself as a media company, as opposed to an organization that created and processed film. Being married to technology puts limits on your ability to grow. As a result, Kodak lost market share to companies like Sony and Instagram. Their fear was leaving profits on the table from their film business. But smart companies launch pilot programs and incubators to shift to new technologies while juicing the old. Instead of Kodak going digital, they attempted to extend the life of print media. But as demand for print regressed, so did their market share.

I'm Not Scared

My mentor, Mark Schaefer, loves to challenge the way professionals think. Mark often talks about the future of business and how technology will change everything. One of his arguments is that AI (artificial intelligence) and writing automation will replace humans. That can be a scary thing for journalists and people who love to write like me. When he first brought this to my attention, I was a bit shocked. My initial thought was, "If robots start doing all the writing, what will I do?" But after inductive reasoning, I realized I could use this technology to my advantage.

Writers have to do a ton of research. However, if we used artificial intelligence to extract the most important information, we would have more time to do other things. This can mean other projects or time with family. My only reservation is being able to put the Larry spin on it. AI will still need someone to tell it what to look for and how to present it.

The Death of Mass Production

With the invention of 3D printing, it is now possible to build just about anything on demand. Makie Labs is one of the first to leverage the technology to do what they call "mass customization." Instead of spending thousands in prototyping, and years of development for one doll, Makie can create a new doll on demand, completely customized from skin tone (including freckles and birthmarks) to hair color and clothing. Everything can be personalized and delivered within weeks.

Technology Revisited

Technology isn't all about apps and gadgets. Technology is any new or better way of doing something. Before email we wrote letters, put them in envelopes, postmarked them, and waited a few days before they were delivered. Why would we do that now? Maybe as a nice gesture. But as a business, why would you waste the time and resources when you can easily send an email in real time?

Jesus Loved Technology

Jesus traveled by boat and wore sandals. He didn't cross the Jordan on a raft, nor did he walk barefoot. He used nets to catch large numbers of fish instead of using hands or spears. He told his disciples to buy swords for defense. He didn't tell them to find rocks and make slings. Are you getting my point?

Technology can make your life easier. If there's an opportunity to reach more, teach more, do more, shouldn't you take advantage?

Netflix: When DVD players started gaining popularity, a good selection of movies was hard to find at your local Blockbuster or Hollywood Video. Out of frustration, a company named Netflix decided to start a DVD by mail service. In 1997, however, DVDs weren't the only thing gaining popularity. The Internet was also starting to look attractive. So the co-founders of Netflix, Reed Hastings and Marc Randolph, decided to create a website that helped you rent movies online and have them mailed within two days. However, most people were out buying DVDs instead of actually renting them. As a result, 97% of all Netflix' revenue came from DVD sales. In an effort to reverse the trend and create a more sustainable business, Netflix decided to stop selling DVDs altogether, and only allowed users to rent. Since Netflix refused to get comfortable with the technology that afforded them their largest profits (the selling of physical DVDs), they positioned their company to grow with the new wave of technology (the Internet). By making people subscribe (instead of just buying one DVD and disappearing), Netflix locked in users by making them members, allowing them to rent an unlimited number of DVDs with no time limits or late fees. This set Netflix up for their digital services that would come later in the future. Blockbuster and Hollywood Video went out of business, however.

The Bible App: In 1996, a company called YouVersion launched its website to help people access the Bible much easier. Other organizations had the same idea. However, by leveraging technology, YouVersion was able to grow much larger and faster than its competitors. By turning their website into an app (known as The Bible App), YouVersion made its product more accessible, allowing it to spread faster and reach further. Accessing the Bible via the Internet was great, but the Bible App was a much better technology that was easier to adopt.

Rebellion

The Only Rule is No Rules

Let's be clear, every industry has its conventions. Without law, there is no challenge. Without challenge, there is no opportunity to be creative. The best work comes from understanding the convention and building on top of it. That's creativity.

For example, basketball legend Lebron James wouldn't be great if it wasn't for conventions. Without rules, there's no way to display creativity. If anything goes, there would be no room for greatness.

Let's say LeBron James and his Cleveland Cavaliers (Cavs) basketball team are down a point in the fourth quarter with 0.5 seconds to go. Steph Curry and Golden State is the challenger, and they just came back from a 10 point deficit. Momentum is on their side. The pressure is on LeBron. The objective is for Cav's Kevin Love to throw an inbound pass to LeBron for a catch and shoot. There's no time to bounce the ball or pass to another player, LeBron has to catch it and dunk it. This will take focus and determination. When it happens, it's glorious, because the objective is nearly impossible to achieve. The convention is time, LeBron only has 0.5 seconds to complete the play. But in the same situation, if LeBron catches the ball, bounces it, hops over three defenders, and jams it backward in 0.6 seconds, it wouldn't matter. You still lose the game because you scored outside the governing rules (time). The play is obsolete.

Are there conventions in marketing? Absolutely. There are conventions in everything. Can these conventions be broken? Absolutely. But it's from understanding the rules that you can effectively break them.

A journalist that writes without flaw, is considered dull. If she really wants to express her creativity, she should bend the rules a little, test the conventions.

Leonardo Da Vinci was a great artist, not because he followed the rules, but because he was great at breaking them. While other Renaissance artists duplicated one another, Da Vinci found ways to create the remarkable by leveraging the conventions of art.

And who can explain Michael Jackson's success. Where the heck did the "moonwalk" come from? Did he actually glide across the stage? That's up for debate. However, he did use the conventions of gravity, time, and natural body movements to create the highly animated dance step.

That's not to say, however, he never broke the rules. The song "Smooth Criminal" addresses abuse. But the way Jackson goes about it is totally unorthodox. Abuse is a very disturbing topic, but there's nothing sad about Smooth Criminal, even though other emotions are present. It boasts an upbeat tempo, a few crotch grabs, spins and kicks. The video, however, uses conventions of storytelling such as a protagonist (Jackson), antagonist (the criminal), inciting event (bar entrance), theme (Armageddon), and narrative (saving the world from abuse).

Yet when you look at Michael Jackson's career, you'll see that his best work was borrowed from the past:

In the song "Wanna Be Startin Somethin'," Jackson borrowed the words "mamase mamasa mamakusa" from the song, "Soul Makossa" by Manu Dibango in 1972.

The moonwalk is a spinoff of "The Buzz," a dance performed by Cab Calloway.

Michael Jackson admitted to stealing from "Can't Go For That," by Hall and Oats, to create "Billie Jean."

And that's what creative people do… build on top of what has already been built.

Wars and Rumors of Wars

And how did Alexander the Great sweep through Asia and Africa devastating armies? If he didn't understand the conventions of warfare, he could have never accomplished his feat. Nevertheless, while his opponents meticulously followed the rules, Alexander defied them and conquered his enemies remaining undefeated in all his battles.

George Washington did something similar. With a smaller army than England, he outsmarted the Brits using guerilla war tactics, driving the nation out and winning America's independence.

Since America has always been underpopulated, we've always relied on technology and unconventional practices to dominate the world. The Internet, B-29 (WWII plane), Apollo 11, and the atomic bomb all came in the midst of much pressure. Each task used conventions to undermine the opposition. How can you build a B-29 without first understanding aerodynamics? You can't, your plane will drop out of the sky.

Jesus was hated because he was so unorthodox, yet he understood the laws better than those who followed them.

The Gospel is disruption at its finest. He spoke about destroying the temple, ending animal sacrifices, and giving women equal rights. This was unheard of in his time and is still an anomaly in some places.

Destroying the holy temple in Jerusalem was like leveling every government building in the United States. Ending animal sacrifices was like ending federal tax. Giving women equal rights was like having a woman dictator in a male-dominated society.

Jesus had a no rules agenda. People were so stuck on the rules, that they missed everything else.

"Look, why are they doing what is unlawful on the Sabbath?" Jesus answered, "Have you never read what David did when he and his companions were hungry and in need?... he entered the house of God and ate the consecrated bread, which is lawful only for priests to eat. And he also gave some to his companions."

Then he said to them, "The Sabbath was made for man, not man for the Sabbath. (Mark 2: 24-27)

Don't Let Conventions Lead You to Death.

When Barak Obama ran for President in 2008, he put his opponents to shame with unconventional wisdom. After Hilary Clinton's defeat to Obama, she came back in 2016 against Trump, campaigning under the ideology that fueled her entire political career. Once again she was devastated by unconventionality. And nobody got it.

The Toyota Way

Toyota teaches its employees to harness the power of contradictions. In 1953, as the smallest auto-maker in the world wanting to compete with larger brands, Toyota made cars on demand, as opposed to using mass production like Ford and GM. This made the quality of their vehicles better, operation less wasteful, and profits much higher. Compared to Ford, Toyota spends six times less to operate with profit margins four times higher.

The Industrial Model Is Dead!

Automobile parts coming down the assembly line, classrooms with 70 seats, Sunday church, toys produced by the thousands, twelve tracks on a compact disc, commercials interrupting TV shows, cars fueled by gasoline, clothing lines… it's all dead! Stop being predictable!

The Resurrection Is Here

There are no gurus, no experts, and no one knows anything. It's all up to you.

No excuses, no debts, no restraints, the only enemy is you.

Everything you need you have. Get started. Produce.

Nothing is new under the sun, yet everything is new for you.

Do Something!

About The Author

Larry C. Lewis grew up in a diverse neighborhood among Christians, Muslims, and Jehovah Witnesses. Despite the religious influence in his life, Larry lived his adolescent years as an atheist. While working towards his Master's degree in marketing, Larry met two friends, Rico and Carlos who opened his mind to Christianity.

But Larry didn't want to be a Christian. In an effort to prove the scriptures wrong he begin to study history, the Bible, and other religious text including the Quran and the Catechism.

Nevertheless, Larry was intrigued by the gospel message. He begins to notice parallels between Jesus' ministry and the marketing campaigns he was taught in school. It was everything from the parables Jesus spoke, to how he built his ministry in the likes of a startup. That's when Larry embraced the idea that nothing is new under the sun.

"It's all just a remix."

You can stay connected with Larry at www.marketinglikeapro.net and by follolowing his adventures on Instagram @larryc_lewis

Made in the USA
Columbia, SC
28 December 2017